Family Stew

A story about two moms who use a sperm donor to build their family.

by Linda Stamm, Psy.D.

Illustrated by Fatima Stamato

For Patricia, Carol, Jenna and Jason,
and all the wonderful mothers who have conceived
their children with the help of a sperm donor.

Olivia lived in a large, white farmhouse with her two cats and her two moms — Momma and Oma. She loved both moms just the same, even though they were very, very different.

When her second grade teacher dismissed class at the end of each day, Olivia felt a spark of excitement in her stomach. Running home, she would hug both of her moms and then spend hours walking around the farm with Oma.

Olivia watched the animals lazily graze in the hills, happily wagging their tails. Oma called to all of the animals, patiently explaining to Olivia how to take care of them.

But when it came to Momma, Olivia often thought,
"She must be the silliest mom in the whole world!"

Momma loved to dance wildly, sing loudly, and tell lots of funny
riddles and jokes to Oma and Olivia. Yet most of all, Momma
loved cooking! She named everything after the food she made...
calling their cow "Cowliflower" and the cats "Marshmallow"
and "Cinnamon." Marshmallow was as white as newly fallen snow
and Cinnamon was as red as a ripe tomato.

Sometimes, Momma even called Olivia, "Olive!"
But Olivia would frown and firmly say,

"Stop it Momma. My name's not Olive. It's Olivia!"

Momma would just giggle
and continue talking.

Momma always said her favorite things to make were stews, stews, stews! To Olivia and Oma, she sometimes spent what seemed like all day talking about her beloved stews. There were her *'crunchy munchy veggie'* and *'flapping codfish'* stews.

One day, Momma turned to Olivia and teased, "How 'bout I make you some scrumptious *'squealing eel'* stew or perhaps *'squirmy wormy octopus'* stew for dinner tonight?"

Momma laughed and laughed.

Olivia turned from Oma to Momma with
her nose scrunched up in a frown and cried,

"No way! Those are '*ooey gooey ooey*' stews!"

And with that, Olivia and Oma ran to her bedroom
and hid under a mountain of covers and pillows
as mysterious, and not so yummy, smells wafted
through the air from the kitchen.

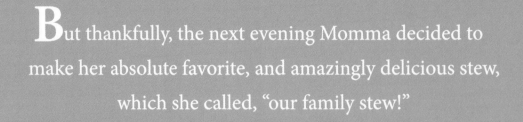

But thankfully, the next evening Momma decided to
make her absolute favorite, and amazingly delicious stew,
which she called, "our family stew!"

Oliva and Oma watched as Momma pranced around the kitchen,
spices flying this way and that, through the air like pixie dust!
She grinned and sang, "A sprinkle of me, a dash of you two,
put it together and you get our family stew!"

Her voice rang out through the kitchen.

And then, as Momma cooked,
she told Olivia their family story.

"Like any good stew, every family is made with its own special
ingredients. Some families have a mom and a dad — others have
one mom or just one dad. Then, there are families with
two dads or, like ours, two moms!"

"When Oma and I fell in love, we were so, so happy,"

Momma's eyes got all dewy and misty as
she glanced at Oma. She continued,
"But we somehow knew we were missing an ingredient…
we needed just one more thing to make the best family stew ever!

We wanted to make a special little baby and have a beautiful boy
or girl!" Oma nodded, adding, "But to make a baby, whether or
not the family has two dads, a mom and dad or two moms…
each one needs to have the same ingredients; an egg from a
woman and a special seed, called a sperm, from a man."

Olivia looked from Oma to Momma, nose crinkled up as
she thought about this. Momma took over explaining again,
"And to make a baby, a woman's egg has to mix with
a man's sperm and then a baby will begin to grow!"

"Well, Oma and I knew we had lots of wonderful eggs between us, but we needed some of those special sperm seeds as well."

Momma paused to sprinkle a dash of some kind of yellow spice into the stew. At this point, Olivia's eyes shifted toward the kitchen pantry, Oma and Momma following her gaze.

Olivia saw all kinds of colorful, different shaped boxes, jars and packages with seeds. There were sesame seeds, pumpkin seeds, and even poppy seeds…but absolutely no sperm seeds!

The confused seven-year-old furrowed her brow and said, "I don't get it, Momma…Oma. I just don't get it."

Momma exchanged a smile with Oma and began to giggle.

Oma put a gentle hand on Olivia's shoulder and said,

"Honey, you can't buy these seeds at a grocery store."

Olivia raised an eyebrow, still a little confused.
Momma spoke up as she dotted
fresh peas into the boiling stew.

"That's right, sweetie! So we went to the doctor
to ask him for help, and he knew exactly where
to find some of these special sperm seeds.
You see, sweet plum, the doctor
knew a very nice man called a donor
who had lots of extra sperm to share."

Olivia rubbed her head, thinking about this as Momma explained more.

"This doctor had a very clever and wonderful idea. He'd take some of the donor's sperm seeds and put them into my stomach…well a place below my stomach called the uterus. And in there, one of the sperm seeds would join one of my eggs, turning into an embryo! That's the teeniest, weeniest beginning of a baby!"

Olivia's eyes grew wide, trying to imagine it all. As Momma smiled and chopped a few onions and carrots, Oma continued explaining in her more matter-of-fact voice.

"You see, the uterus is a sack inside women, which all of our girl animals like the cows and sheep have as well. In the uterus an embryo can grow properly."

Olivia nodded, though she didn't really understand.

Momma tried to explain in less technical terms.

"Sweetie, it was like, well, like a little warm oven where the embryo that would become you stayed cozy, safe and healthy inside me…that is until you were ready to come out and become the delicious little bean sprout you are today!"

Momma finished with a laugh. Even Oma let out a giggle as Olivia looked back and forth between her moms, mouth gaped open! Olivia's wonder soon turned to a frown along with an eye roll at Momma.

"Oh Momma, I'm not a bean sprout, thank you very much!"

Oma laughed even harder along with Momma, who said, "You know, you're right. You're my yummy little Olive!"

"It took weeks and weeks, seasons changed, and my belly got bigger and bigger as you grew! When that day finally arrived, when you were born, Oma and I cried and cried with joy!"

Oma wanted to add a few more details, saying,

"And Olivia, the science is actually extraordinary… each egg and sperm have genes in them."

Oliva looked down at the blue jeans she wore, one eyebrow raised in disbelief. Oma smiled and shook her head.

"No, not those kinds of jeans."

Before Oma could continue, Momma explained,

"They're kind of like little lists of ingredients for a recipe… one that makes you look like you! But you also got a lot of who you are from growing up with Oma and me!"

Olivia stared at the bubbling stew that now filled the room with mouth-watering aromas. Finally, she looked at Momma and said,

"Do we know where the donor man is?"

For once, Momma grew serious and said,

"No sweetie, the donor is anonymous, which means we don't know his name or where he lives. But we do know that he has brown hair and blue eyes just like you. And he's studying at school to become a veterinarian. Like that doctor that helps take care of all our animals when they're sick."

This made Olivia grin — she loved all of the animals on the farm and thought that the animal doctor was cool.

Momma still looked serious.

"Maybe when you're all grown up into a beautiful young lady, we'll get to know more about him."

Olivia looked from Momma, whose mouth formed a straight line, to Oma, whose eyes looked almost tear-filled. Olivia was puzzled, thinking hard about everything. Then, the corners of Momma's mouth started to curl into a big round smile. Before Olivia could blink an eye, Momma was dancing and singing again.

"A little pinch of us and a dash of him and you…
mix it all together and we'll make a family stew!"

This time Oma and Olivia ran to hug Momma,
dancing along with her. The three of them fell giggling to the floor,
into a big bowl of yummy tickle stew!

Don't miss these other titles by the same author!

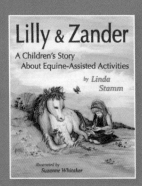

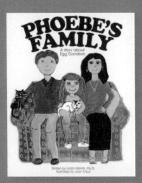

Dr. Linda Stamm, Psy.D. has been a practicing clinical psychologist for more than 20 years, first in Boston and now in Atlanta. She specializes in the assessment and treatment of psychological issues related to infertility, pregnancy, perinatal loss and the postpartum period.

In her private practice, she provides psychotherapy to individuals, couples and groups, and routinely serves as a consultant to several reproductive endocrinology clinics.

Dr. Stamm received her bachelor's degree in psychology from Brown University and her doctorate in clinical psychology from Rutgers University.

Printed in Great Britain
by Amazon

16247871R00016